Mother Teresa:
Quotes & Facts

By Blago Kirov

First Edition

I0412966

*****

Mother Teresa: Quotes & Facts
*****

Table of Contents

Yesterday is gone.
Tomorrow has not yet come.
We have only today.
Let us begin.

Foreword

This book is an anthology of 201 quotes from Mother Teresa and selected facts about Mother Teresa.

Teresa of Calcutta (1910-1997) with secular name Agnes Gonxha Bojaxhiu, and also known as St. Teresa of Calcutta or Mother Teresa of Calcutta, was a Catholic nun of Albanian origin naturalized Indian, who founded the congregation of the Missionaries of Charity in Calcutta in 1950. For more than 45 years she cared for the poor, the sick, orphans and the dying, while guiding the expansion of her congregation, first in India and then in other countries around the world.

Her canonization was approved by Pope Francis on December 2015, after the Congregation for the Causes of Saints recognized as extraordinary the healing of a terminally ill Brazilian. The official act of canonization took place in Rome on the morning of Sunday, September 4, 2016.

Agnes discovered her vocation at an early age, and by 1928 had decided that she was destined for religious life. It was then that she chose to change her name to "Teresa" in honor to the patron saint of missionaries, Therese of Lisieux. Although she spent the next 20 years teaching in the Irish convent of Loreto, she began to care for the sick and the poor of the city of Calcutta. This led her to found a congregation to help the marginalized in society, primarily the sick, the poor, and the homeless.

By the 1970s she was internationally known and had acquired a reputation as a humanitarian and advocate for the poor and defenseless, in part because of Malcolm Muggeridge's documentary and book Something Beautiful for God. Mother Teresa won the Nobel Peace Prize in 1979 and India's highest civilian award, the Bharat Ratna, in 1980, for her humanitarian work. They were joined by a dozen top-level national and international awards and recognitions.

She received praise from many individuals, governments, and organizations. However, she also faced several criticisms, such as the objections of Christopher Hitchens, Michael Parenti, Aroup Chatterjee and the World Hindu Council, which blamed her for a reactionary mentality and criticized the insufficient attention in her centers. In 2010, the anniversary of her birth, she was honored around the world, and her work praised by Indian President Pratibha Patil.

Her Words

"Everything that is not given is lost."

"Peace begins with a smile."

"Yesterday is gone. Tomorrow has not yet come. We have only today. Let us begin."

"I fear just one thing: Money! Greed was what motivated Judas to sell Jesus"

"We are all pencils in the hand of God."

"Work without love is slavery."

"A beautiful death is for people who lived like animals to die like angels—loved and wanted."

"A clean heart is a free heart. A free heart can love Christ with an undivided love in chastity, convinced that nothing and nobody will separate it from his love. Purity, chastity, and virginity created a special beauty in Mary that attracted God's attention."

"A joyful heart is the normal result of a heart burning with love. She gives most who gives with joy."

"A life not lived for others is not a life."

"A sacrifice to be real must cost, must hurt, and must empty ourselves. Give yourself fully to God. He will use you to accomplish great things on the condition that you believe much more in his love than in your weakness."

"Am I ever angry or frustrated? I only feel angry sometimes when I see waste, when things that we waste are what people need, things that would save them from dying. Frustrated? No, never."

"And if we accept that a mother can kill even her own child, how can we tell other people not to kill one another? How do we persuade a woman not to have an abortion? As always, we must persuade her with love and we remind ourselves that love means to be willing to give until it hurts. Jesus gave even His life to love us. So, the mother who is thinking of abortion, should be helped to love, that is, to give until it hurts her plans, or her free time, to respect the life of her child. The father of that child, whoever he is, must also give until it hurts."

"And so let us always meet each other with a smile, for the smile is the beginning of love..."

"Any country that accepts abortion is not teaching its people to love but to use violence to get what they want."

"As for me, the silence and the emptiness is so great, that I look and do not see, — Listen and do not hear — the tongue moves but does not speak ... I want you to pray for me — that I let Him have free hand."

"As soon as we take the enfleshment of God, the incarnation which, for Christians, is represented by the person of Jesus Christ, then we start taking things seriously."

"At the end of life we will not be judged by how many diplomas we have received, how much money we have made, how many great things we have done.
We will be judged by "I was hungry, and you gave me something to eat, I was naked and you clothed me. I was homeless, and you took me in."

"At the hour of death when we come face-to-face with God, we are going to be judged on love; not how much we have done, but how much love we put into the doing."

"Be faithful in small things because it is in them that your strength lies."

"Be happy in the moment, that's enough. Each moment is all we need, not more."

"Being unwanted, unloved, uncared for, forgotten by everybody, I think that is a much greater hunger, a much greater poverty than the person who has nothing to eat."

"But still, everything is for Jesus; so like that everything is beautiful, even though it is difficult."

"Cheerfulness is a sign of a generous and mortified person who forgetting all things, even herself, tries to please her God in all she does for souls. Cheerfulness is often a cloak which hides a life of sacrifice and a continual union with God."

"Christ came to be Father's compassion to the world. Be kind in your actions. Do not think that you are the only one who can do efficient work, work worth showing. This makes you harsh in your judgment of others who may not have the same talents. Do your best and trust that others do their best. And be faithful in small things because it is in them that your strength lies."

"⬆ Discipline is the bridge between goals and accomplishment."

"Do not think that love in order to be genuine has to be extraordinary. What we need is to love without getting tired. Be faithful in small things because it is in them that your strength lies."

"Do not wait for leaders; do it alone, person to person."

"Do small things with great love."

"Don't look for big things, just do small things with great love...the smaller the thing, the greater must be our love."

"Each of us is merely a small instrument; all of us, after accomplishing our mission, will disappear."

"Each one of them is Jesus in disguise."

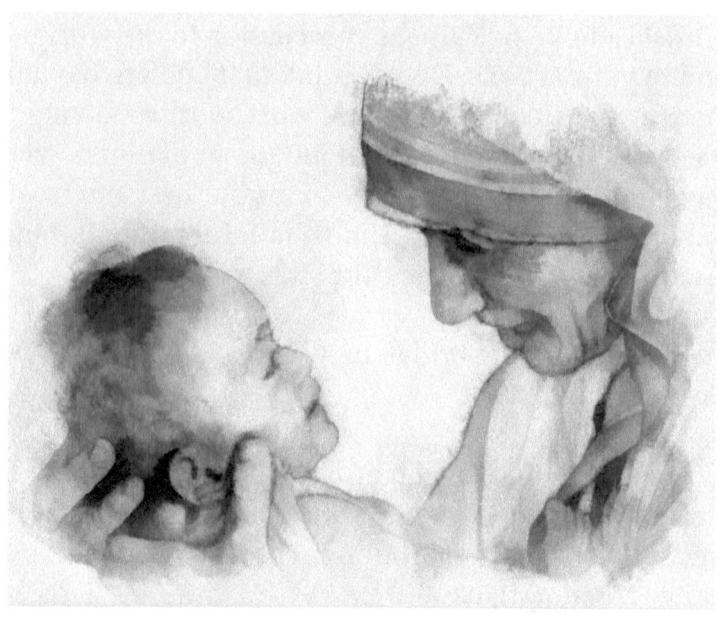

"Do we know our poor people? Do we know the poor in our house, in our family? Perhaps they are not hungry for a piece of bread. Perhaps our children, husband, wife, are not hungry, or naked, or dispossessed, but are you sure there is no one there who feels unwanted, deprived of affection?"

"Even if you're on the right track, you'll get run over if you just sit there."

"Every time you smile at someone, it is an action of love, a gift to that person, a beautiful thing."

"Faith is a gift from God and he gives it to whomever he chooses"

"Give that child to me. I want it. I will care for it. I am willing to accept any child who would be aborted and to give that child to a married couple who will love the child and be loved by the child."

"Give, but give until it hurts."

"Go out into the world today and love the people you meet. Let your presence light new light in the hearts of people."

"God doesn't ask that we succeed in everything, but that we are faithful. However beautiful our work may be, let us not become attached to it. Always remain prepared to give it up, without losing your peace."

"God doesn't require us to succeed; he only requires that you try."

"God gives us things to share; God doesn't give us things to hold..."

"God made the world for the delight of human beings--if we could see His goodness everywhere, His concern for us, His awareness of our needs: the phone call we've waited for, the ride we are offered, the letter in the mail, just the little things He does for us throughout the day. As we remember and notice His love for us, we just begin to fall in love with Him because He is so busy with us -- you just can't resist Him. I believe there's no such thing as luck in life, it's God's love, it's His."

"Good works are links that form a chain of love"
Mother Theresa"

"He has told us that He is the hungry one. He is the naked one. He is the thirsty one. He is the one without a home. He is the one who is suffering. These are our treasures, she said, looking at the rows of pallets in the caravanserai. They are Jesus."

"He who is faultless does not care for the opinion of others."

"Holiness does not consist in doing extraordinary things. It consists in accepting, with a smile, what Jesus sends us. It consists in accepting and following the will of God."

"How can there be too many children? That is like saying there are too many flowers."

"Humility is the mother of all virtues; purity, charity and obedience. It is in being humble that our love becomes real, devoted and ardent. If you are humble nothing will touch you, neither praise nor disgrace, because you know what you are. If you are blamed you will not be discouraged. If they call you a saint you will not put yourself on a pedestal."

"Hungry for love, He looks at you. Thirsty for kindness, He begs of you. Naked for loyalty, He hopes in you. Homeless for shelter in your heart, He asks of you. Will you be that one to Him?"

"I alone cannot change the world, but I can cast a stone across the waters to create many ripples."

"I am a little pencil in God's hands. He does the thinking. He does the writing. He does everything and sometimes it is really hard because it is a broken pencil and He has to sharpen it a little more."

"I am but a small pencil in the hand of a writing God"

"I am not sure exactly what heaven will be like, but I know that when we die and it comes time for God to judge us, he will not ask, 'How many good things have you done in your life?' rather he will ask, 'How much love did you put into what you did?"

"I can do things you cannot, you can do things I cannot; together we can do great things."

"I do not pray for success, I ask for faithfulness."

"I feel the greatest destroyer of peace today is 'Abortion', because it is a war against the child... A direct killing of the innocent child, 'Murder' by the mother herself... And if we can accept that a mother can kill even her own child, how can we tell other people not to kill one another? How do we persuade a woman not to have an abortion? As always, we must persuade her with love... And we remind ourselves that love means to be willing to give until it hurts..."

"I go of my free choice, with the blessing of obedience."

"I have found the paradox that if I love until it hurts, then there is no hurt, but only more love."

"I have more often as my companion "darkness." And when the night becomes very thick- and it seems to me as if I will end up in hell- then I simply offer myself to Jesus."

"I hope that what you give me comes not from your surplus but it is the fruit of a sacrifice made for the love of God. You must give what costs you, go without something you like, then you will truly be brothers to the poor who are deprived of even the things they need."

"I know God won't give me anything I can't handle. I just wish he didn't trust me so much."

"I must be willing to give whatever it takes to do good to others. This requires that I be willing to give until it hurts. Otherwise, there is no true love in me, and I bring injustice, not peace, to those around me."

"I pray that you will understand the words of Jesus, "Love one another as I have loved you." Ask yourself "How has he loved me? Do I really love others in the same way?" Unless this love is among us, we can kill ourselves with work and it will only be work, not love. Work without love is slavery."

"I prefer you to make mistakes in kindness than work miracles in unkindness."

"I still think that the greatest suffering is being lonely, feeling unloved, just having no one... That is the worst disease that any human being can ever experience."

"I think it is very good when people suffer. To me that is like the kiss of Jesus. "

"I want you to be concerned about your next door neighbour. Do you know your next door neighbour?"

"I was once asked why I don't participate in anti-war demonstrations. I said that I will never do that, but as soon as you have a pro-peace rally, I'll be there."

"I will never understand all the good that a simple smile can accomplish."

"I would rather make mistakes in kindness and compassion than work miracles in unkindness and hardness."

"If I look at the mass I will never act."

"If our bones were not sending whispers of doubt to our hearts, there would be no need for prayer at all."

"If we accept that a mother can kill her own child, how can we tell other people not to kill each other? Any country that accepts abortion is not teaching its people to love, rather, to use violence to get what they want."

"If we have no peace, it is because we have forgotten that we belong to each other."

"If we pray, we will believe; If we believe, we will love; If we love, we will serve."

"If we want a love message to be heard, it has got to be sent out. To keep a lamp burning, we have to keep putting oil in it."

"If you are humble nothing will touch you, neither praise nor disgrace, because you know what you are."

"I see Jesus in every human being. I say to myself, this is hungry Jesus, I must feed him. This is sick Jesus. This one has leprosy or gangrene; I must wash him and tend to him. I serve because I love Jesus."

"If we really want to love we must learn how to forgive."

"If you are kind, people may accuse you of selfish, ulterior motives: Be kind anyway. If you are successful you will win some false friends and true enemies: Succeed anyway. If you are honest and frank people will try to cheat you: Be honest anyway. What you spend years building, someone could destroy overnight: Build anyway. If you find serenity and happiness, they may be jealous of you: Be happy anyway. The good you do today, will often be forgotten by tomorrow: Do good anyway. Give the world the best you have, and it may never be enough: Give your best anyway."

"If you can't feed a hundred people, feed just one."

"If you do good, people will accuse you of selfish ulterior motives. Do good anyway."

"If you give what you do not need, it is not giving."

"If you judge people, you have no time to love them."

"In light of heaven, the worst suffering on earth, a life full of the most atrocious tortures on earth, will be seen to be no more serious than one night in an inconvenient hotel."

"In loving one another through our works we bring an increase of grace and a growth in divine love."

"In the developed countries there is a poverty of intimacy, a poverty of spirit, of loneliness, of lack of love. There is no greater sickness in the world today than that one."

"In the final analysis it is between you and God, it was never between you and them anyway."

"In the home begins the disruption of the peace of the world."

"In the silence of the heart God speaks. If you face God in prayer and silence, God will speak to you. Then you will know that you are nothing. It is only when you realize your nothingness, your emptiness, that God can fill you with Himself. Souls of prayer are souls of great silence."

"In the West we have a tendency to be profit-oriented, where everything is measured according to the results and we get caught up in being more and more active to generate results. In the East -- especially in India -- I find that people are more content to just be, to just sit around under a banyan tree for half a day chatting to each other. We Westerners would probably call that wasting time. But there is value to it. Being with someone, listening without a clock and without anticipation of results, teaches us about love. The success of love is in the loving -- it is not in the result of loving.

"Intense love does not measure it just gives."

"It is a kingly act to assist the fallen."

"It is poverty to decide that a child must die so that you may live as you wish."

"It is easy to love the people far away. It is not always easy to love those close to us. It is easier to give a cup of rice to relieve hunger than to relieve the loneliness and pain of someone unloved in our own home. Bring love into your home for this is where our love for each other must start."

"It is not how much we do, but how much love we put in the doing. It is not how much we give, but how much love is put in the giving."

"It is not the magnitude of our actions, but the amount of love that is put into them that matters."

"It is not what to do, but how much love we put into the doing. We can do not greats, only small things with great love."

"It's not how much we give but how much love we put into giving."

"Jesus announced which will be the criteria of the final judgment of our lives: we will be judged according to love.We will be judged according to the poor of spirit or money."

"Jesus said love one another. He didn't say love the whole world."

"Jesus wants me to tell you again...how much is the love He has for each one of you-beyond all what you can imagine...Not only He loves you, even more--He longs for you. He misses you when you don't come close. He thirsts for you. He loves you always, even when you don't feel worthy..."

"Joy is a net of love in which you can catch souls."

"Joy is a sign of generosity. When you are full of joy, you move faster and you want to go about doing good to everyone."

"Joy is strength."

"Joy must be one of the pivots of our life. It is the token of a generous personality. Sometimes it is also a mantle that clothes a life of sacrifice and self-giving. A person who has this gift often reaches high summits. He or she is like sun in a community."

"Keep the corners of your mouth turned up. Speak in a low, persuasive tone. Listen; be teachable. Laugh at good stories and learn to tell them...For as long as you are green, you can grow."

"Kind words can be short and easy to speak, but their echoes are truly endless."

"Let no one ever come to you without leaving better and happier. Be the living expression of God's kindness: kindness in your face, kindness in your eyes, kindness in your smile."

"Let us always meet each other with smile, for the smile is the beginning of love."

"Let us make one point, that we meet each other with a smile, when it is difficult to smile. Smile at each other, make time for each other in your family."

"Let us not be satisfied with just giving money. Money is not enough, money can be got, but they need your hearts to love them. So, spread your love everywhere you go."

"Let us touch the dying, the poor, the lonely and the unwanted according to the graces we have received and let us not be ashamed or slow to do the humble work."

"Life is an opportunity, benefit from it. Life is beauty, admire it. Life is a dream, realize it. Life is a challenge, meet it. Life is a duty, complete it. Life is a game, play it. Life is a promise, fulfill it. Life is sorrow, overcome it. Life is a song, sing it. Life is a struggle, accept it. Life is a tragedy, confront it. Life is an adventure, dare it. Life is luck, make it. Life is too precious, do not destroy it. Life is life, fight for it."

"Like Jesus we belong to the world living not for ourselves but for others. Give yourself fully to God. He will use you to accomplish great things on the condition that you believe much more in His love than in your own weakness."

"Live simply so others may simply live."

"Loneliness and the feeling of being unwanted is the most terrible poverty."

"Loneliness is the leprosy of the modern world."

"Love begins at home, and it is not how much we do... but how much love we put in that action"

"Love begins by taking care of the closest ones - the ones at home."

"Love is a fruit in season at all times and within reach of every hand."

"Love is not patronizing and charity isn't about pity, it is about love. Charity and love are the same -- with charity you give love, so don't just give money but reach out your hand instead."

"Love to be real, it must cost—it must hurt—it must empty us of self."

"Love until it hurts."

"May God break my heart so completely that the whole world falls in."

"Never be so busy as not to think of others."

"Never travel faster than your guardian angel can fly."

"Never worry about numbers. Help one person at a time and always start with the person nearest you."

"Not all of us can do great things. But we can do small things with great love."

"One filled with joy preaches without preaching."

"One of the greatest diseases is to be nobody to anybody"

"Our life of contemplation shall retain the following characteristics: — missionary: by going out physically or in spirit in search of souls all over the universe. — contemplative: by gathering the whole universe at the very center of our hearts where the Lord of the universe abides, and allowing the pure water of divine grace to flow plentifully and unceasingly from the source itself, on the whole of his creation. — universal: by praying and contemplating with all and for all, especially with and for the spiritually poorest of the poor."

"Our poor people are great people, a very lovable people, They don't need our pity and sympathy. They need our understanding love and they need our respect. We need to tell the poor that they are somebody to us that they, too, have been created, by the same loving hand of God, to love and be loved."

"Pain and suffering have come into your life, but remember pain, sorrow, suffering are but the kiss of Jesus - a sign that you have come so close to Him that He can kiss you."

"People are unreasonable, illogical, and self-centered. Love them anyway. If you do good, people may accuse you of selfish motives. Do good anyway. If you are successful, you may win false friends and true enemies. Succeed anyway. The good you do today may be forgotten tomorrow. Do good anyway. Honesty and transparency make you vulnerable. Be honest and transparent anyway. What you spend years building may be destroyed overnight. Build anyway. People who really want help may attack you if you help them. Help them anyway. Give the world the best you have and you may get hurt. Give the world your best anyway."

"Persuaded of our nothingness and with the blessing of obedience we attempt all things, doubting nothing, for with God all things are possible. We will allow the good God to make plans for the future, for yesterday has gone, tomorrow has not yet come, and we have only today to make him known loved, and served. Grateful for the thousands of opportunities Jesus gives us to bring hope into a multitude of lives by our concern for the individual sufferer, we will help our troubled world at the brink of despair to discover a new reason to live or to die with a smile of contentment on its lips."

"Poverty was not created by God. It is we who have caused it, you and I through our egotism."

"Prayer in action is love, love in action is service."

"Profound joy of the heart is like a magnet that indicates the path of life."

"See how nature - trees, flowers, grass - grows in silence; see the stars, the moon and the sun, how they move in silence...we need silence to be able to touch souls."

"Prayer is not asking. Prayer is putting oneself in the hands of God, at His disposition, and listening to His voice in the depth of our hearts."

"Prayer is the mortar that holds our house together."

"Prayer makes your heart bigger, until it is capable of containing the gift of God himself. Prayer begets faith, faith begets love, and love begets service on behalf of the poor."

"Seeking the face of God in everything, everyone, all the time, and his hand in every happening; This is what it means to be contemplative in the heart of the world. Seeing and adoring the presence of Jesus, especially in the lowly appearance of bread, and in the distressing disguise of the poor."

"She knows how to suffer and at the same time how to laugh."

"Smile at each other. Smile at your wife, smile at your husband, smile at your children, smile at each other- it doesn't matter who it is- and that will help to grow up in greater love for each other."

"Some people come in our life as blessings. Others come in our life as lessons."

"Sometimes a good feeling from inside is worth much more than a beautician."

"Spread love everywhere you go: first of all in your own home. Give love to your children, to your wife or husband, to a next door neighbour . . . Let no one ever come to you without leaving better and happier. Be the living expression of God's kindness; kindness in your face, kindness in your eyes, kindness in your smile, kindness in your warm greeting."

"Spread love everywhere you go. Let no one ever come to you without leaving happier."

"Spread the love of God through your life but only use words when necessary."

"Suffering is nothing by itself. But suffering shared with the passion of Christ is a wonderful gift, the most beautiful gift, a token of love."

"The fruit of faith is love, and the fruit of love is service...spread love everywhere u go.."

"The fruit of silence is prayer, the fruit of prayer is faith, the fruit of faith is love, the fruit of love is service and the fruit of service is peace."

"The good you do today may be forgotten tomorrow. Do good anyway. Give the world the best you have and it may never be enough. Give your best anyway. For you see, in the end, it is between you and God. It was never between you and them anyway."

"The greatest destroyer of peace is abortion."

"The greatest mistake is to think you are too strong to fall into temptation. Put your finger in the fire and it will burn. So we have to go through the fire."

"The greatest disease in the West today is not TB or leprosy; it is being unwanted, unloved, and uncared for. We can cure physical diseases with medicine, but the only cure for loneliness, despair, and hopelessness is love. There are many in the world who are dying for a piece of bread but there are many more dying for a little love. The poverty in the West is a different kind of poverty - it is not only a poverty of loneliness but also of spirituality. There's a hunger for love, as there is a hunger for God."

"The greatest science in the world; in heaven and on earth; is love."

"The hunger for love is much more difficult to remove than the hunger for bread."

"The more you have, the more you are occupied, the less you give. But the less you have the more free you are. Poverty for us is a freedom. It is not mortification, a penance. It is joyful freedom. There is no television here, no this, no that. But we are perfectly happy."

"The most terrible poverty is loneliness, and the feeling of being unloved."

"The person who gives with a smile is the best giver because God loves a cheerful giver."

"The so-called right to abortion has pitted mothers against their children and women against men. It has sown violence and discord at the heart of the most intimate human relationships. It has aggravated the derogation of the father's role in an increasingly fatherless society. It has portrayed the greatest of gifts-- a child--as a competitor, an intrusion and an inconvenience. It has nominally accorded mothers unfettered dominion over the dependent lives of their physically dependent sons and daughters. And, in granting this unconscionable power, it has exposed many women to unjust and selfish demands from their husbands or other sexual partners."

"The success of love is in the loving - it is not in the result of loving. Of course it is natural in love to want the best for the other person, but whether it turns out that way or not does not determine the value of what we have done."

"The trees, the flowers, the plants grow in silence. The stars, the sun, the moon move in silence. Silence gives us a new perspective."

"The very fact that God has placed a certain soul in our way is a sign that God wants us to do something for him or her. It is not chance; it has been planned by God. We are bound by conscience to help him or her."

"The way you help heal the world is you start with your own family."

"There are many people who can do big things, but there are very few people who will do the small things."

"There is a light in this world, a healing spirit more powerful than any darkness we may encounter. We sometimes lose sight of this force when there is suffering, too much pain. Then suddenly, the spirit will emerge through the lives of ordinary people who hear a call and answer in extraordinary ways."

"There is a terrible hunger for love. We all experience that in our lives - the pain, the loneliness. We must have the courage to recognize it. The poor you may have right in your own family. Find them. Love them."

"There is thing you can do but I can not and there is thing I can but you can not; so let us - together - make something beautiful for God."

"There should be less talk; a preaching point is not a meeting point. What do you do then? Take a broom and clean someone's house. That says enough."

"There's nothing more calming in difficult moments that knowing there's some one fighting with you."

"To keep a lamp burning, we have to keep putting oil in it."

"To the good God nothing is little because He is so great and we so small- that is why He stoops down and takes the trouble to make those little things for us- to give us a chance to prove our love for Him."

"Today somebody is suffering, today somebody is in the street, today somebody is hungry. ... We have only today to make Jesus known, loved, served, fed, clothed, sheltered. Do not wait for tomorrow. Tomorrow we will not have them if we do not feed them today."

"We cannot do great things on this Earth, only small things with great love."

"We do not need guns and bombs to bring peace, we need love and compassion."

"We know only too well that what we are doing is nothing more than a drop in the ocean. But if the drop were not there, the ocean would be missing something."

"We learn humility through accepting humiliations cheerfully."

"We must know that we have been created for greater things, not just to be a number in the world, not just to go for diplomas and degrees, this work and that work. We have been created in order to love and to be loved."

"We need to find God, and he cannot be found in noise and restlessness. God is the friend of silence. See how nature - trees, flowers, grass- grows in silence; see the stars, the moon and the sun, how they move in silence... We need silence to be able to touch souls. "

"We the willing, led by the unknowing, are doing the impossible for the ungrateful. We have done so much, with so little, for so long, we are now qualified to do anything, with nothing."

"We think sometimes that poverty is only being hungry, naked and homeless. The poverty of being unwanted, unloved and uncared for is the greatest poverty. We must start in our own homes to remedy this kind of poverty."

"We too are called to withdraw at certain intervals into deeper silence and aloneness with God, together as a community as well as personally; to be alone with Him — not with our books, thoughts, and memories but completely stripped of everything — to dwell lovingly in His presence, silent, empty, expectant, and motionless. We cannot find God in noise or agitation."

"What can you do to promote world peace? Go home and love your family."

"What you spend years building may be destroyed overnight; build it anyway."

"When a poor person dies of hunger it has not happened because God did not take care of him or her. It has happened because neither you nor I wanted to give that person what he or she needed."

"When you don't have anything, then you have everything."

"When you have nothing left but God, you have more than enough to start over again."

"When you know how much God is in love with you then you can only live your life radiating that love."

"Without patience, we will learn less in life. We will see less. We will feel less. We will hear less. Ironically, rush and more usually mean less."

"Words which do not give the light of Christ increase the darkness."

Some Facts about Mother Teresa

Early years

Agnes Gonxha Bojaxhiu ('Gonxha' means 'pink bud' or 'small flower' in Albanian).

She was born on August 26, 1910, in Uskub, at that time part of the Ottoman Empire, and today in Skopje, Northern Macedonia. However, the date of her birth considered being August 27, as this is the day she was baptized.

She was the youngest child born in a successful marriage between Nikollë Bojaxhiu (1878-1919) and Dranafile Bernai (1889-1972).

Her family belonged to the Albanian ethnic group of Kosovo. Her father was probably from Prizren and her mother from a village near Gjakova.

Her father was involved in Albanian politics. He died suddenly and mysteriously in 1919 when Agnes was only eight years old. He was hospitalized for a sudden illness but is suspected of having been poisoned.

After his death, Agnes' mother raised her and taught her the norms of the Catholic religion. "I am an Albanian of blood and origin. Through my vocation, I belong to the whole world, but my heart belongs entirely to Jesus," Mother Teresa will say later.

In her childhood, Agnes attended public school and participated as a solo soprano in a parish choir. In the absence of the conductor, she even conducts the choir.

She belonged to the Congregation of the Marianas, founded in 1563 and known as Sodalicio de Nuestra Señora.

There she became interested in the stories of the Jesuit missionaries from Yugoslavia who were sent to Bengal. From that time on, she has endeavored to work in India just as she did. Already at a young age, Agnes was fascinated by the life stories of the missionaries and their affairs in Bengal.

She received her First Communion at the age of 5 and her confirmation at the age of six.

When she was twelve years old, she was already convinced that she should devote herself to religion. Her final decision was made on August 15, 1928, when she prayed in the chapel of Virgen Negra de Letnice, a place where she often worshiped.

On September 26, 1928, shortly after her 18th birthday, she went with a friend to the Loreto Abbey, a Catholic community of the Institute of the Virgin Mary, in Rathfarnham, Ireland.

From now on, she will never see her mother or sister again.

Initially, she visited this place intending to learn English as this is the language in which the Loreto Sisters teach children in India.

After being accepted as a candidate, she moved to Calcutta by sea on January 6, 1929. She began her mission in Darjeeling, near the Himalayas.

She learned Bengali while teaching English at the Santa Teresa School near her monastery.

After confessing to poverty, chastity, and submission as a nun on May 24, 1931, she was transferred to Santa Maria College in Entali, east of Calcutta.

At that time she chose the name of Thérèse de Lisieux, patron saint of the missionaries. However, since another nun of the Methodist had already chosen this name, Agnes decided to use the word with his Castilian name Teresa instead of Thérèse.

On May 14, 1937, Teresa made her solemn vows when she taught at the Methodo School in Loreto. She worked there as a teacher of history and geography and became director of the center in 1944.

While she enjoys teaching at school, she feels increasingly embarrassed and saddened by the poverty in Calcutta. The 1943 famine in Bengal brought misery and death to the city. In August 1946 a wave of Hindu-Muslim violence broke out in the town, plunging the population into despair and terror.

Missionaries of Charity

On September 10, 1946, Mother Teresa experienced what she later described as "the voice of enlightenment from above." It happened when she took the train to Loreto Monastery in Darjeeling, Calcutta. "I had to leave the monastery and help the poor while I lived among them. It was a commandment. Later, on this occasion, Joseph Langford wrote: "Sister Teresa now becomes "Mother Teresa."

Teresa began missionary work with the poor in 1948. This reflected in her appearance that she replaced her traditional nun's clothes, which she wore in Loreto, with a white cotton sari with a blue-collar.

Teresa accepts Indian citizenship. She spends several months in Patna to receive necessary medical training at the Holy Family Hospital and visits to impoverished areas. Teresa founded a school in Motijhil, Kolkata before taking care of the poor and starving.

In early 1949, Teresa joined the efforts of a group of young women and created a new religious community to help the "poorest of the poor."

Their efforts quickly attracted the attention of Indian officials, including the Prime Minister.

She wrote in her diary that her first year was challenging. Without income she asks for food and supplies and for uncertainty, loneliness and the temptation to return to the comfort of the monastery in those early months: "Our Lord wants me to be a free nun who has carried the cross of poverty. Today I have learned a good lesson. The poverty of the poor is so bad for them. As I searched for a home, I went and walked until my hands and feet hurt. I thought how much more painful than this body pain is the pain of the soul for those who are seeking for a home, food, and sustenance. " You only have to say the word and everything you had there will be yours again," Tempter whispered to me. By choice, my God, and by love for you, I want to stay and do whatever your holy will is for me. I have not allowed a single tear in my eyes. "

On October 7, 1950, Teresa received permission from the Vatican for her diocesan Congregation to become Missionaries of Charity. Its primary purpose was to care for the " starving, naked, homeless, mutilated, blinds, and lepers, all those who feel unwanted, unloved, disabled in the whole of society, who have become a burden of the nation and are avoided by it all."

By 1997, the 13-member community in Calcutta had grown to more than 4,000 sisters running AIDS hospices, orphanages, and charity centers around the world. They care for refugees, the blind, the disabled, the elderly, alcoholics, the poor, and the homeless, as well as victims of floods or epidemics, and famine.

In 1952 she opened her first hospice with the help of government officials from Calcutta. She transformed the abandoned Hindu temple into a Kalighat home for the dying, renamed it Nirmal Hriday and made it a free and unrestricted entrance for the poor. The inhabitants of the house received medical help and the opportunity to complete their earthly journey with dignity according to their faith. Muslims read lines from the Koran, Hindus received water from the Ganges and Catholics received their last anointing. "Beautiful Death," Teresa says, "is one in which people who lived as animals die as angels - loved and desired."

She opened a hospice for lepers and called it Shanti Nagar (City of Peace). The Missionaries of Charity set up leprosy clinics throughout Calcutta, supplying them with medicines, bandages, and food.

The Missionaries of charity have taken care of more and more homeless children. By 1955, Teresa Nirmala found Shishu Bhavan, the children's home of the Immaculate Heart, as a refuge for orphans and homeless youth.

The community began to attract volunteers and donations and opened hospices, orphanages and leprosy clinics throughout India in the 1960s. Teresa then expanded the Congregation abroad and opened a house in Venezuela with her five sisters in 1965. Homes in Italy (Rome), Tanzania and Austria followed in 1968. In the 1970s, the Congregation opened houses and foundations in the USA and other countries in Asia, Africa, and Europe.

The Missionaries of Charity Brothers was founded in
1963, followed by the contemplative branch of the
Sisters in 1976. Catholics and non-Catholics are
enrolled in Mother Teresa's staff. In response to the
request of many priests, Mother Teresa founded the
Corpus Christi Movement for Priests in 1981.

Together with priest Joseph Langford, they founded Missionaries of Charity Fathers in 1984. They want to combine the professional goals of Missionaries of Charity with the resources of the priesthood. Until 2007, missionaries of charity counted about 450 brothers and 5,000 sisters worldwide. They run a total of 600 missions, schools and shelters in 120 countries around the world.

I belong to the world

Teresa says to herself, " I am Albanian by blood. By nationality, Indian. By faith, I am a Catholic nun. As for my vocation, I belong to the world. As for my heart, I belong entirely to the Heart of Jesus. "

She spoke five languages - Bengali, Albanian, Serbian, English, and Hindi. This led her to travel regularly outside India for humanitarian reasons.

At the pick of the siege of Beirut in 1982, she rescued thirty-seven children trapped in a front hospital. This happened through a temporary ceasefire between the Israeli army and the Palestinian guerrillas. Accompanied by Red Cross workers, she crossed the war zone to the hospital to evacuate young patients at risk of her life.

As Eastern Europe gained more freedom and openness in the late 1980s, Mother Teresa extended her efforts to the former communist countries that had previously rejected her missionaries of charity.

Regardless of the criticism of her position, she has launched dozens of projects against abortion and divorce: "No matter who says what, you have to accept it with a smile and do the job," she comments on the criticism.

Teresa visited Armenia after the 1988 earthquake and met with Nikolai Ryzhkov, the chairman of the USSR Council of Ministers.

Teresa traveled to Africa to help the starving in Ethiopia, but she did not forget the victims of Chernobyl radiation and the victims of the earthquake in Armenia.

In 1991 Teresa returned to Albania for the first time and opened the home of Missionaries of Charity Brothers in Tirana.

By 1996, Teresa had launched 517 missions in over 100 countries. Her charity missionaries increased their number from twelve in the beginning to thousands. These missions serve the "poorest of the poor" in 450 centers around the world.

The first home of the Missionaries of Charity in the USA is located in the South Bronx, New York. Until 1984, the church operated 19 facilities across the country.

Poor Health and Her Death

She had a heart attack in Rome in 1983 when she visited Pope John Paul II.

After the second outbreak in 1989, she began to live with an artificial pacemaker.

In 1991 she had additional heart problems after a pneumonia attack in Mexico.

Although Teresa has proposed her resignation as leader of the Missionaries of Charity, the sisters of the Council vote by secret ballot for her to remain in office and she agrees to continue.

In April 1996, she collapsed and fractured her collarbone. Four months later, he fell ill with malaria and heart failure.

Although Teresa underwent heart surgery, her health began to deteriorate.

According to Calcutta's Archbishop Henry Sebastian D'Souza, he ordered a subordinate priest to carry exorcism to Terese. This came with her permission until she was hospitalized for the first time with heart problems. The decision was made because the Archbishop believed that the devil might have attacked Teresa.

On March 13, 1997, Teresa resigned as director of the Missionaries of Charity.

She died on September 5, just five days after the death of another of the world's most famous women, Lady Diana Spencer.

At the time of her death, Missionaries of Charity had over 4,000 sisters and an associated brotherhood of 300 members who completed 610 missions in 123 countries. Their responsibilities include hospices and homes for people with HIV/AIDS, leprosy and tuberculosis patients, free soup kitchens, children and family counseling programs, and schools.

Missionaries of Charity is supported by volunteer co-workers, who numbered over one million until the 1990s.

One week before the funeral, Teresa's body lies in public service in an open coffin in St. Thomas, Calcutta.

She receives a government-sponsored funeral from the Indian government in gratitude for her service to the poor of all religions in the country.

With the support of five other priests, the last funeral service was conducted by Cardinal Secretary of State Angelo Sodano, while a representative of the Pope personally performed the final rituals.

Secular and religious communities lament Teresa's death. Pakistan's Prime Minister Nawaz Sharif called her "a rare representative of humanity, a unique person who dedicates her entire life to higher purposes. Her commitment to caring for the poor, sick, and disadvantaged is one of the best examples of serving our humanity. "

According to Javier Pérez de Cuéllar: "Teresa is the U.N. herself. She is world peace."

Recognition, respect, and criticism

The Indian government first recognized Teresa for more than 30 years before her death. In 1962 she received the Padma Shri and in 1969 the Jawaharlal Nehru Prize for International Understanding.
She later received other Indian awards, including Bharat Ratna, which was the highest civilian award in India in 1980.

Teresa's official biography, written by Navin Chawla, was published in 1992.

In Calcutta, she is still worshipped by some Hindus as a goddess.

To celebrate the 100th anniversary of Teresa's birth, the Indian government had issued a commemorative coin — the same amount of money Teresa had when she arrived alone in India.

On August 28 2010, Indian President Pratibha Patil said: "Mother Teresa and the Sisters of the Missionaries of Charity, wearing a white sari with a blue-collar, have become a symbol of hope for many, elderly, needy, unemployed, sick and terminally ill people and those who have been abandoned by their families."

However, Hindi reviewers of Teresa were not only favorable or superior. Aroup Chatterjee, a doctor, born and raised in Calcutta who worked in urban areas until 1980 before moving to Britain, said he "never saw nuns in these poor areas." His research includes more than 100 interviews with volunteers, nuns, and others familiar with the Missionaries of Charity. He published all these interviews in a separate book in 2003, which criticized Teresa. In this book, the author Chatterjee criticizes Teresa for promoting a "cult of suffering." Also, Teresa has created a distorted, negative image of Calcutta, which overstates the significance of the work done by her mission. According to him, she also used the resources and privileges with which she carried out her duties as head of mission. Finally, in his opinion, as a health care provider, some hygiene issues, such as the reuse of needles, were not resolved until after Teresa's death in 1997.

Bikash Ranjan Bhattacharya, Mayor of Calcutta from 2005 to 2010, said that "it had no significant impact on poverty alleviation in this city." He accuses her of healing illnesses and suffering instead of really curing them. Also, Mother Teresa misrepresented the city. Without a doubt, there was poverty in Calcutta," he writes, "but this city has never been a city of lepers and beggars, as Teresa expressed it."

In Hindu political system, the Bharatiya Janata Party is also opposed to Teresa. The representative of this party, Mr. Christian Dalits, publicly praised her at the funeral service and sent a representative to her funeral. Another representative of the same party, Vishwa Hindu Parishad, spoke out against the government's decision to grant her a state funeral.

Secretary Giriraj Kishore said: "Mother Teresa was primarily committed to the Church, and her social service was secondary and marginal." This politician also accuses her of benefiting only Christians and of carrying out "secret baptisms" of those who are dying.

An introductory article in the Hindi weekly Frontline rejected the allegations against Mother Teresa as "clearly false" and said that these allegations "had no impact on the Indian society's view of her work, especially on the people of Calcutta." The author of the editorial in the newspaper praised her " altruistic care, energy, and courage " and yet criticized Teresa's public campaign against abortion.

In February 2015, Mohan Bhagwat, chairman of the right-wing Hindu organization Rashtriya Swayamsevak Sangh, declared that Teresa's goal was "to transform anyone she helped into a Christian." Former RSS spokesman M.G. Vaidhya supported Bhagwat's assessment, and his organization accused the Indian media of "falsifying the facts about Mother Teresa."

Delhi Prime Minister Arvind Kejriwal strongly protested against Mohan Bhagwat's statement.

In 1962 Teresa was awarded the Ramon Magsaysay Prize for Peace and International Understanding for her work in South and East Asia. The congratulations before the award ceremony read: "The Board of Trustees appreciates her compassionate attitude towards the poor and needy in a foreign country in which she is leading her congregation."

In the early 1970s, she was already an international celebrity. Teresa's fame can be attributed in part to Malcolm Muggeridge's 1969 documentary film Something Beautiful for God and his book of the same name from 1971.

During the shooting of some of his footage in poor light conditions in the dormitory, he felt that they could not be used due to their bad quality. In England, however, the film crew found the footage exceptionally well lit and Muggeridge calls this a miracle caused by the "divine light" emanating from Teresa.

However, other team members tell him that this is due to a new type of Kodak film that is sensitive to ultrasound, rather than to "divine light."

Later, after the broadcast of his film, Muggeridge changed his faith in Catholicism.

Around this time, the Catholic world began to worship Teresa publicly. In 1971 Pope Paul VI awarded her with the Opening Prize and Pope John XXIII with the Peace Prize. He praised her work with the poor, her Christian charity and her efforts for peace on the planet.

Mother Teresa received the Pacem in Terris Award in 1976.

She was honored as an honorary recipient by governments and civil society organizations and nominated in 1982 as an Australian Order Volunteer Associate "Serving the Community of Australia and Humanity in General."

Teresa's Albanian homeland awarded her with the nation's Golden Honor in 1994.

Despite her high honors, she was controversially received by the media along with the Haitian Legion of Honor Award. Teresa was criticized for implicitly supporting the dictator Duvaliers and corrupt businessmen such as Charles Keating and Robert Maxwell. The last charge related to the fact that she wrote to the judge at the Keating trial, asking him for forgiveness.

Universities in India and the West have also awarded her honorary degrees.

Other popular awards included the Balzan Prize for the Promotion of Humanity, Peace, and Brotherhood among Peoples (1978) and the Albert Schweitzer Prize (1975).

In April 1976 she visited the University of Scranton in northeastern Pennsylvania, where she was awarded the La Storta Medal for Human Service by University President William J. Byron. She calls upon an audience of 4,500 people to "know the needs of poor people in their own homes and neighborhoods," to "feed these poor and hungry people, or simply spread joy and love among them." Finally, in her famous speech, she says: "The poor will help us to grow spiritually in holiness, for they are Christ Himself, hidden under the veil of suffering."

In August 1987, Teresa was awarded an honorary doctorate in social sciences for her services to the poor and sick. She then spoke with over 4,000 students and members about her service to the "poorest of the poor" and invited her listeners to "do the little things with great love."

The United Kingdom and the US have awarded Mother Teresa with many prizes. Their culmination was the award of the Order of Merit in 1983 and the grant of honorary citizenship of the US on 16 November 1996.

In 1979 Mother Teresa received the Nobel Peace Prize "for her work in the fight against poverty and suffering, which are also a great threat to peace."

She rejected the conventional Nobel Prize and demanded that the cost of the $192,000 banquet be made available to the poor in India. Teresa justified her claim by saying that Earth's rewards were only essential to her if they would help her serve the world's needy.

When Teresa received the Nobel Prize, Teresa was asked:
"What can we do to promote world peace?
She replied, "Go home and love your families."

In her Nobel lecture on receiving the award, she said: "Worldwide, not only in poor countries, but I have also found poverty in the West, which is much more difficult to eliminate than that of the East."

Teresa quotes abortion as "the greatest destroyer of peace today. Because if a mother can kill her child, it merely means that there is nothing between them, the love bond is broken. "

Barbara Smoker of the liberal world magazine The Freethinker criticized Teresa after receiving the Nobel Peace Prize. Smoker said that Teresa's promotion of Catholic moral doctrines about abortion and contraception had drawn funds from other effective methods of solving India's problems.

At the Fourth World Conference on Women in Beijing, Mother Teresa said: "People can destroy this gift of motherhood, primarily through the evil caused by abortion. This is what we do, and we think that there are other things like work or career that are more important than love. "

Throughout her life, Teresa was consistently among the top 10 women in the annual survey of the most influential Gallup men and women 18 times.

According to a document by Canadian scientists Serge Larivée, Geneviève Chénard, and Carole Sénéchal, Teresa's clinics received million-dollar donations but still lacked medical care, systematic diagnosis, nutrition, and sufficient pain relief. According to these three scholars, "Mother Teresa believed that the sick, like Christ, should suffer on the cross." Canadians say in their study that the extra money could have improved the health of the poor in the city by creating modern palliative care centers, but that did not happen in practice.

One of Teresa's most outspoken critics is the English journalist, writer, and atheist Christopher Hitchens. He is the author of the documentary The Angel of Hell (1994) and the author of Mother Teresa in Theory and Practice (1995).

Christopher Hitchens wrote in an article published in 2003: "This media uproar over Mother Teresa brings us back to the Medieval corruption of the Church, which sold indulgences to the rich while preaching hellish fire and torment for the poor. Mother Teresa was not a friend of the poor, and she was a friend of poverty. She said that suffering was a gift from God. She spent her life resisting the only known means against poverty, namely to empower women and free them from their predestined role as breeding animals."

Christopher Hitchens accused Teresa in hypocrisy in her choice of technologically advanced treatment of heart disease. Hitchens stated that "her intention was not to help people" and that she had lied to donors about how her contributions were used. "When I spoke to her, I found out, and Teresa also assured me that she was not working to alleviate poverty," he says. "Teresa works mainly to increase the number of Catholics. She told me: 'I am not a social worker. That's why I don't do it. I do it for Christ. I do it for the Church." Hitchens' accusations are dangerous but mostly manipulative and therefore unfounded. This is because he tells only part of the truth about Mother Teresa, the part that resonates with his personal political beliefs.

Although Hitchens thought he was the only witness called by the Vatican, Aroup Chatterjee, author of Mother Teresa: The Untold Story, was also asked to produce evidence that violated Teresa's beatification and canonization. The Vatican has eliminated the traditional "devil's advocate" of the institution who served it for a similar purpose but instead referred to persons like Teresa's two public opponents. In their case, their arguments do not support the weight of their claims.

Abortion rights groups also criticize Teresa's attitude to abortion and contraception.

Melanie McDonagh believes that Mother Teresa is widely "criticized for not being what she never wanted to be, that is, for having done things she has never seen in her work." "Mother Teresa was not a social worker, she argues. - She did not have the illusion of being able to eliminate the root causes of poverty. "She wanted to do nothing more than stand with people in the lower parts of society as if she were Christ Herself."

Mari Marcel Thekaekara points out that after the war in Bangladesh, several million refugees from former East Pakistan have been expelled to Calcutta. "No one has ever done anything like Mother Teresa to take people in need and dying off the sidewalks and give them a clean and holy place to die with dignity."

Navin B. Chawla points out that Mother Teresa never intended to build hospitals, but to create a place where those who were denied all access to society could "at least die in peace and with a peaceful soul and leave the earthly world with dignity." He also rejected accusations that regular hospitalizations in her organization were motivated by her desire for secret baptisms in the Catholic faith. "Those who are in a hurry to criticize Mother Teresa and her mission cannot or will not do anything for these people to help them with their own hands," he writes.

According to Mark Woods, an author of Christian Today: "And perhaps just as crucial for her public perception is the feeling among Christians that her critics don't understand what she's doing. For example, if she is criticized for her rejection of abortion and contraception, it means criticizing her for not running a secular charity that she never pretended to wish. "

In some individual cases, Mother Teresa also undertook uncompromising asceticism based on her deep and uncompromising faith. This is the case, for example, when she refuses to accept a large building in the New York Bronx as a donation to create a homeless shelter. When the city council decided to install an elevator for the disabled under a condition determined by them, and Mother Teresa rejected that condition, the entire project was rejected and failed. She justifies these decisions with the words: "God did not call us to be successful and effective, but to be faithful to Him."

"Dark Night of the Soul"

Pope John Paul II analyzed her actions and successes and said: "Where did Mother Teresa find the strength and tenacity to serve others fully? She discovered this strength in prayer and the silent contemplation of Jesus Christ, his Holy Face, his Sacred Heart. "

Mother Teresa experienced her doubts and spiritual struggles in her religious faith on her own. This inner struggle lasted almost 50 years, for the rest of her life. According to her Vatican postulator Brian Kolodiejchuk, "she sometimes felt no presence of God ... in her heart or the Eucharist, she had her moments of weakness."

Teresa expresses her severe doubts about the existence of God and her pain due to lack of faith. "Where is my faith? - she writes. - Also deep in my soul ... nothing but emptiness and darkness ... If there is a God - please forgive me. When I try to raise my thoughts to heaven, I see such a forceful emptiness there that these thoughts come back as sharp knives and hurt my soul." Kolodiejchuk, the official representative of the Vatican, who collects evidence of her canonization, believes that some may misinterpret her thoughts. He writes that her belief that God works through her always remains intact and healthy. Although she had trouble regaining her lost closeness to God, she never questioned His existence. Teresa, he believes, might have experienced something similar to Jesus saying on the cross: "Eli Eli lama sabachthani? ("My God, my God, why have you forsaken me?")

To make her motives even more transparent, Kolodiejchuk compares them with the mystic John of the Cross from the 16th century, to whom the phrase "Dark Night of the Soul" belongs. Other saints, including Teresa's namesake Thérèse of Lisieux, who also spoke "Night of Nothingness," had similar experiences of spiritual emptiness.

According to James Langford, these doubts were typical of bright minds and souls and did not prevent the canonization of these men and women before Teresa. After ten long years of uncertainty, Teresa herself described her short period of renewed faith. After the death of Pope Pius XII in 1958, she prayed for him in the Requiem Mass, when she was suddenly freed from the "long darkness: from this strange suffering." Five weeks later, her spiritual emptiness returned.

Over a long period of 66 years, Teresa wrote numerous letters to her confessors and superiors, in particular to the Archbishop of Calcutta, Ferdinand Perier, and the Jesuit priest Celeste van Exem. The latter had been her spiritual advisor since the founding of Missionaries of Charity.

In her last will, she demanded the destruction of her letters and feared that "people would think more of me and less of Jesus." However, her correspondence was collected in Mother Teresa: Come, be my light.

We can read there that, for example, Teresa writes to the spiritual confidant Michael van der Peett: "Jesus has an extraordinary love for you. But for me, the silence and emptiness are so high that I look and do not see - listen and do not hear - my tongue moves in prayer, but I do not speak ... I want you to pray for me so that I can communicate with Him through my deeds. "

In Deus Caritas Est, titled his first encyclical, Pope Benedict XVI mentions Mother Teresa three times and uses the description of her life to illustrate one of the main points of his encyclical: "Using the example of the blessed encyclical of Calcutta, we have a clear example of the fact that the Time dedicated to God in prayer not only interferes with the practical and loving service of our neighbor but is also an inexhaustible source of this service. "

Mother Teresa writes: "Only through spiritual prayer and spiritual reading can we promote the gift of praying."

Although her Order was not related to the Franciscan Orders, Mother Teresa admired Francis of Assisi. The spirituality of the Franciscans influenced her. The Sisters of Charity recited St. Francis' prayer at each morning liturgy. Moreover, their emphasis on service and many of their vows are similar to those of the Franciscans. For example, Saint Francis also emphasized the poverty, chastity, the obedience, and devotion of Christ. He dedicated a large part of his life to the service of the poor, especially the lepers.

Beatification

After the death of Teresa in 1997, the Holy Throne began the process of canonization, the second of the three steps to canonization. For this purpose, Kolodiejchuk was appointed postulator by the Calcutta Diocese. Although he states: "We should not have proved that she was perfect or had never made a mistake ...", he must prove that Teresa's virtue is a spiritual achievement.

Kolodiejchuk presents 76 documents with a total volume of 35,000 pages, based on interviews with 113 witnesses who were asked to answer 263 questions. The process of canonization requires the documentation of a miracle resulting from the deeds of the future saint.

In 2002, the Vatican confirmed the wound healing of a tumor in the belly of an Indian woman, Monica Besra, after attaching a medallion with a photo of Teresa. According to Besra, the light was radiated from the photo, and her cancer tumor was cured. However, her husband and some of her medical staff said that only conventional medical treatment had removed cancer. Dr. Ranjan Mustafi, who said in an interview with The New York Times that he was treating Besra, testified that the cyst was caused by tuberculosis: "It was no wonder ... he says:" She took medication for nine months to a year. "

According to Besra's husband: "My wife was healed by doctors, not by a miracle ... This miracle is a joke."

Besra herself reports that her medical records, including sonograms, prescriptions and doctors' notes, were confiscated by Sister Betta from the Missionaries of Charity. According to Time, phone calls to Sister Betta and the service of Sister Nirmala, Teresa's successor as Director of the Order, received no response or comment. Officials at Balurghat Hospital, where Besra sought medical treatment, said they had been pressured by the Order to call the patient a "miracle cure."

During the beatification and canonization of Teresa, the Roman Curia (Vatican) studied all published and unpublished critiques of her life and work. Hitchens and Chatterjee, the author of The Final Verdict, a book critical of Teresa, spoke before the Vatican Tribunal. Vatican representatives say the Congregation is investigating the accusations for the Cause of the Saints. The group found no obstacle to the canonization of Teresa and issued its nihil obstat on April 21, 1999. In a separate medical panel, it was decided that Monica Besra's miracle, one of the three wonders considered by Kolodiejchuk, was proof of divine advocacy. So Teresa was finally beatified on October 19, 2003, and revealed to Catholics as "blessed."

On December 17, 2015, the Vatican Press Service confirmed that Pope Francis acknowledges a second miracle attributed to Teresa: the healing of a Brazilian man with multiple brain tumors in 2008.

Francis canonized her at a ceremony on September 4, 2016, at St. Peter's Square. The ceremony was witnessed by tens of thousands, including 15 government delegations and 1,500 homeless people from all over Italy. The event was broadcast live on the Vatican channel and online.

Teresa's hometown announced a week-long celebration of its canonization.

In India, the canonization was celebrated with special Mass by the Missionaries of Charity in Calcutta. On September 4, 2017, Sister Mary Prema Pierick, Superior General of the Missionaries of Charity, announced on the occasion of the first anniversary of her canonization that Archbishop Teresa would assume patronage of the Archdiocese of Calcutta during Holy Mass in the Cathedral of the Holy Rosary. The next day, Archbishop Thomas D'Souza, who heads the Roman Catholic Archdiocese of Calcutta, confirmed that Teresa, together with Francis Xavier, would be appointed Patroness of the Diocese of Calcutta. Teresa is mentioned by museums and is the patron saint of many churches.

Mother Teresa Day (Dita e Nënë Terezës) on October 19 is an official holiday in Albania.

In 2009, the Mother Teresa Memorial Home was opened in her home town of Skopje, Northern Macedonia.

The Roman Catholic Cathedral in Pristina in Kosovo is named after her.

Mother Teresa Women's University in Kodaikanal was founded in 1984 by the Tamil Nadu government as a state university.

The Mother Teresa Institute of Health Sciences in Pondicherry was founded in 1999 by the government of Puducherry.

The Sevalaya charity runs the Mother Teresa Girl Home, where poor and orphaned girls near the village of Kasuva in Tamil Nadu receive free food, clothing, shelter, and education.

Since September 5, 2013, the United Nations General Assembly has declared the day of her death to be the International Day of Charity.

On September 5, 2017, the Cathedral of Saint Teresa, the first Roman Catholic cathedral named in honor of Teresa, is inaugurated in Kosovo. The cathedral is also the first Roman Catholic cathedral in Kosovo.

Teresa is the theme of the 1969 documentary and the 1972 book Something Beautiful for God by Malcolm Muggeridge. The film manages to draw the attention of the Western world to Mother Teresa.

Geraldine Chaplin played Teresa in Mother Teresa: In the Name of the Poor of God, which was awarded the Art Film Festival Prize in 1997.